INTERNATIONAL PATENT PROTECTIONS FOR SMALL BUSINESSES

UNITED STATES PATENT AND TRADEMARK OFFICE

I0475817

CONTENTS

Section Title				*Page*
EXECUTIVE SUMMARY				1
I.	**INTRODUCTION**			4
II.	**BACKGROUND**			5
	A.	Methodology		5
	B.	Responsiveness		6
III.	**DISCUSSION**			6
	A.	Findings		6
		1.	Patenting in U.S. small businesses is relatively uncommon, and concentrated in high technology sectors	7
		2.	Patenting can be important to the competitiveness of small businesses	8
		3.	Internationalization strategies can facilitate small business growth and job creation	9
		4.	Patent protection abroad opens opportunities for successful entry into global markets	10
		5.	Small businesses may be obtaining patent protection abroad less frequently than large companies	12
			a. Case Study: Traffic Surveillance Technology	15
			b. Case Study: Scanning and Imaging Technology	15
		6.	International patenting costs are often substantial	16
		7.	Patenting expenses often occur early in the life of small businesses and are difficult to fund	19
		8.	Foreign countries largely take a different approach than the United States in assisting small businesses to acquire patent protection	22
		9.	In response to the questions presented by Congress, the USPTO has identified points of agreement among respondents and witnesses as to what the U.S. Government can do to help small businesses with international patent protection	24

a.   The U.S. Government should engage in diplomacy and harmonization to reduce the costs associated with filing foreign patent applications 25

b.   The U.S. Government should approach the direct subsidizing of foreign patenting costs with care 26

c.   The U.S. Government should pursue an aggressive program of education for small businesses on foreign patenting 27

10.   In continued response to the questions presented by Congress, the USPTO offers some observations regarding loan programs and grant programs 28

B.   Recommendations 29

1.   The U.S. Government should engage in diplomacy and harmonization to reduce the costs associated with filing foreign patent applications 29

2.   The USPTO and SBA should partner in an expanded IP education and training initiative aimed at American small businesses 30

3.   The USPTO and SBA should engage industry to discuss how best to support U.S. small business efforts to patent internationally 31

4.   The USPTO and SBA should collect more information and conduct more study on the most appropriate methods of supporting international patenting by small businesses 32

IV.   **CONCLUSION** 33

EXECUTIVE SUMMARY

Background

Recent economic research shows that small businesses are the primary driver of job creation in the United States, with young startup companies, which are by their nature small businesses, creating on average three million U.S. jobs per year. Though this pattern of job creation has largely held true for over thirty years, the capacity of American small businesses to create jobs is at risk. American firms compete and grow by supplying products and services that consumers demand, and by internationalizing their businesses through licensing, franchising, or exporting. For many small companies, patent protection prevents competitors from simply copying their innovations, and aids in attracting investor capital needed to grow, build market share, and create jobs. Yet small companies face significant financial challenges in acquiring, maintaining, and enforcing patents outside the United States. Therefore, supporting small firms and fostering job creation requires a thorough understanding of these challenges and an exploration of possible remedies.

The Leahy-Smith America Invents Act requires the Director of the United States Patent and Trademark Office, in consultation with the Secretary of Commerce and the Administrator of the Small Business Administration, to study how best to support businesses with international patent protection. The USPTO and SBA are required to determine whether a revolving fund loan program or a grant program would be proper for helping small businesses defray the costs of filing, maintaining, and enforcing international patents. The USPTO and SBA are required to provide other pertinent recommendations.

To prepare this report, the USPTO principally relied upon input from the public, seeking comments through a *Federal Register* notice and holding two public hearings to collect evidence for this study. At each hearing, government panelists from the USPTO and SBA invited and accepted formal testimony, and allowed informal comment and questioning from members of the public. In all, the USPTO received eighteen sets of comments, including responses from a U.S. intellectual property organization, an international industry organization, a foreign government intellectual property office, a U.S. law firm, a U.S. private company, eight U.S. patent practitioners, and five American citizens speaking as individuals. In addition, the USPTO conducted research, relying upon archival sources such as reports, economic studies, and existing data sources where available.

Findings

Available information, including the comments and testimony that the USPTO received, indicates that while patenting appears relatively uncommon among U.S. small businesses, it tends to be concentrated in high technology companies and can aid in securing for them a competitive advantage.

1

Many small companies grow and create new jobs by following an internationalization strategy, and in this regard international patenting – when done early in the life of a company – can provide a platform for tapping new markets later in life. Evidence also suggests that U.S. small businesses may be patenting less frequently than larger firms, and that they face high costs in pursuing international patent protection. These high patenting costs often occur early in the life of these companies, when funding and cash flows are generally limited. These international patenting costs are also often exacerbated for U.S. small companies because – unlike the USPTO, which gives discounts to eligible small businesses from all over the world – foreign patent offices do not generally provide discounts for small businesses.

Commentary and evidence recognized that other governments around the world are subsidizing patenting by their citizens, with China being the largest and most aggressive actor in this regard. However, public comments reflected considerable skepticism as to whether the U.S. government ought to provide public funding to small businesses for international patenting, instead generally favoring market solutions where possible. Comments agreed overwhelmingly with the proposition that the U.S. Government should engage in diplomacy and patent-system harmonization to help reduce the costs associated with filing foreign patent applications. Moreover, there was general agreement that an aggressive program of small-business education could aid American companies to make informed decisions regarding the optimal international patent strategy. Consistent with the public's reluctance to support government financing, there was no consensus as to whether a revolving loan program or a grant program would be more appropriate.

Recommendations

This report's findings support the notion that many small businesses may benefit from extending patent rights outside the U.S., but too few are aware of the need to do so or the pathways and mechanisms that are available to make these decisions accurately and pursue them cost effectively. To improve awareness and expertise among small businesses, the USPTO and the SBA are positioned to build upon several successful current intellectual property education and training programs. One such program is the USPTO's Intellectual Property Awareness Campaign, focusing on intellectual property basics and offered since 2005 to over a thousand small businesses in various cities throughout the U.S. To reach more small businesses, it may be productive to scale up the current IPAC program through existing partnerships between the USPTO and SBA. The USPTO also recommends ongoing industry engagement to investigate useful approaches to solving the issues raised in this report, including possibly public-private partnerships or other means of helping small businesses.

Public commentary also supports the notion that the public is uncertain about whether the U.S. government should use taxpayer dollars to directly subsidize small business foreign patenting in place of market solutions. There is too little evidence upon which to base sound policy in this area: Neither the academic research nor public comment offered sufficient evidence to determine relative advantages, if any, of the U.S. government employing a loan versus a grant program to help defray the expenses of small businesses seeking international patent protection. Given the lack of data, USPTO does not recommend a program of taxpayer-funded financial assistance to support small business foreign patenting at this time. However, it would be useful and informative as a next step for the USPTO, the SBA, and other allied agencies to collect more information.

I.   INTRODUCTION

While firms of all sizes create jobs, recent research shows that small businesses are the primary driver of job creation in the United States. In fact, a relatively small number of American businesses create a disproportionately large share of new jobs. One recent study finds that fewer than five percent of U.S. companies may create more than two-thirds of American jobs, and that these companies on average employ only 61 workers in a given year.[1] Other economic research suggests that young startup companies, which are by their nature small businesses, create an average of 3 million jobs per year, far more than their larger counterparts. This pattern has held generally in the U.S. for more than three decades.[2]

Disturbingly, current economic research shows that these contributions by America's small businesses are at risk. One study found that U.S. small businesses are beginning to generate fewer jobs than would be expected from the historical trend.[3] This study finds that the nature of new, generally small, businesses is changing and moving in the direction of providing less employment. This study also finds that the trend predates the recession that began in 2007. Thus, although small firms remain substantial job creators, their contributions cannot be taken for granted.

American businesses compete and grow in marketplaces by supplying products and services that consumers demand, and by internationalizing their businesses through licensing, franchising, or exporting. For innovators in the American economy, patent protection is often necessary to prevent copying and help in attracting investor capital, thereby allowing these companies to make the necessary investments to grow, build market share, and create jobs. For U.S. small businesses trying to compete in global markets, securing patent protection overseas can be a critical precondition to successfully internationalizing and developing into the productivity powerhouses of tomorrow. Yet small businesses also face significant challenges—particularly financial challenges—in acquiring, maintaining, and enforcing patents abroad. Therefore, supporting small businesses and fostering job creation requires understanding these challenges and exploring possible remedies.

The Leahy-Smith America Invents Act ("AIA") requires the Director of the United States Patent and Trademark Office ("USPTO" or "Office"), in consultation with the Secretary of Commerce and the Administrator of the Small Business Administration ("SBA"), to study how the USPTO, in coordination

---

[1] *See* Magnus Henrekson & Dan Johansson, *Gazelles as Job Creators - A Survey and Interpretation of the Evidence* (Research Institute of Industrial Economics, Working Paper No. 733, 2008), *available at* http://ssrn.com/abstract=1092938.

[2] *See* Tim J. Kane, *The Importance of Startups in Job Creation and Job Destruction* (July 2010), *available at* http://ssrn.com/abstract=1646934.

[3] *See* E.J. Reedy & Robert E. Litan, *Starting Smaller; Staying Smaller: America's Slow Leak in Job Creation* (July 2011), *available at* http://ssrn.com/abstract=1883660.

with other Federal departments and agencies, can best support businesses with international patent protection. The USPTO is directed to make a determination as to whether a revolving fund loan program or a grant program should be established to help small businesses defray the costs of filing, maintaining, and enforcing international patents. The USPTO may also provide to Congress any other pertinent legislative recommendations.[4]

II. BACKGROUND

A. Methodology

In order to obtain statistically rigorous evidence regarding the questions posed by Congress, the USPTO attempted to design and conduct a primary survey of small businesses about their patenting practices. However, the Office was required to complete the study in four months from enactment of the AIA and was permitted to use only its existing resources. These requirements foreclosed the ability to conduct a primary survey of small businesses inquiring about the challenges in patenting outside the U.S. To overcome a lack of information about the extent of the problem, staff in the USPTO Office of Chief Economist analyzed data gathered from the National Science Foundation's 2008 Business R&D and Innovation Survey ("BRDIS"), conducted in early 2009 and housed at the U.S. Census Bureau. Analysis of these data did not, however, support the reporting of any robust inferences regarding the importance of foreign patenting to small businesses or the relationship of foreign patenting to several economic performance measures of interest. Still, the Office was able to gather a number of studies and reports that examined issues related to the questions raised by Congress, but found only a limited body of literature directly examining the questions posed in the legislation. The pertinent findings of this existing literature are discussed below.

In order to report on the key issues, the Office principally sought and relied upon input from the public. Specifically, the Office published a Federal Register notice seeking comments and announcing two public hearings for this study.[5] The Office also provided the public with a dedicated e-mail address and a contact person in the USPTO Office of Chief Economist to receive comments and answer questions. As announced in a Federal Register publication, the Office held two public hearings, one at the USPTO headquarters in Alexandria, Virginia, on Thursday, October 27, 2011, and another at the University of Southern California Gould School of Law in Los Angeles, California, on Tuesday, November 1, 2011. At both hearings, witnesses provided testimony and exchanged comments with the

---

[4] Leahy-Smith America Invents Act, Pub. L. No. 112-29, § 31, 125 Stat 284, 339-40 (2011).
[5] Request for Comments and Notice of Public Hearings on the Study of International Patent Protection for Small Businesses, 76 Fed. Reg. 62,389, 62,391 (Oct. 7, 2011).

audience in person as well as via teleconference. Representatives from both the USPTO and SBA attended the hearings and actively questioned witnesses. At each hearing, government panelists from the USPTO and SBA also invited and accepted spontaneous formal testimony, and allowed informal commenting and questioning from members of the public.

B. Responsiveness

Through the *Federal Register* notice and hearings, the Office received eighteen sets of comments and testimony.[6] Respondents and witnesses included a U.S. intellectual property organization, an international industry organization, a foreign government intellectual property office, a U.S. law firm, a U.S. private company, eight U.S. patent practitioners, and five American citizens speaking as individuals.

III. DISCUSSION

A. Findings

The academic literature, comments, and testimony that the Office received and reviewed indicate that patenting activity is relatively uncommon among small businesses and, where it does occur, is concentrated in high technology sectors. There is evidence in the literature as well as agreement among respondents that patenting and internationalization can be significant drivers of competitiveness and growth, and boost the job creation potential of a small business. Indeed, patent protection was identified as a key factor to many successful entries into global markets. Yet despite these rewards from international patent protection, American small businesses may be patenting abroad less frequently than larger, more established firms.

Public comments suggest that the reasons why small businesses may be patenting abroad less frequently are largely economic and driven by liquidity constraints faced by many small businesses early in life. International patenting costs can run in the hundreds of thousands of dollars,[7] a substantial expense given the limited resources of many small businesses and start-up firms. Moreover, patenting expenses often occur early in the life of small businesses. At these early stages of innovation and development, such high costs are also likely the most difficult to fund. The result is an often intractable choice for some

---

[6] *See* Public Comments for International Protection for Small Business Study, *available at* http://www.uspto.gov/aia_implementation/intl_patent_protection.jsp, Transcript of Public Hearing on the Study of International Patent Protection for Small Businesses: Hearing Before USPTO & SBA (Oct. 27, 2011) [hereinafter "USPTO Hearing"], *available at* http://www.uspto.gov/aia_implementation/111027-ipsb_transcript.pdf, *and* Transcript of Public Hearing on the Study of International Patent Protection for Small Businesses: Hearing Before USPTO & SBA (Nov. 1, 2011) [hereinafter "USC Hearing"], *available at* http://www.uspto.gov/aia_implementation/111101-ipsb_transcript.pdf.

[7] Comments of Biotechnology Industry Organization, at 3, *available at* http://www.uspto.gov/aia_implementation/ipp-2011oct20-bio.pdf.

small firms and independent inventors: to succeed, they can neither ignore international patent protection nor afford it.

Against this problem, the approach of the United States is mostly different from that of other countries. The United States, by providing discounted filing and maintenance fees for small businesses and independent inventors regardless of national origin or industry, takes an impartial, technology-neutral approach that supports innovation by the smallest economic players. By contrast, most other countries do not offer financial support to small entities through discounted filing and maintenance fees, and those that do often use direct subsidies and other government aid that singles out particular firms and industries for support rather than impartial, technology-neutral support. Many such aid programs restrict the application of these benefits to their domestic applicants, to the detriment of American small businesses that seek to compete globally.

1.   **Patenting by U.S. small businesses is relatively uncommon, and concentrated in high technology sectors.**

Unfortunately, the United States does not have a full picture of how, and under what circumstances, small businesses are using the patent system, whether domestically or internationally. The USPTO has recorded huge increases in the numbers of patent applications being filed at the Office, a trend that reflects both the increasing innovativeness of society and also the value of intellectual property protection in a global economy more and more defined by the production of intangible assets. U.S.-origin patent applications submitted to the USPTO grew from 177,511 in 2001 to 241,977 in 2010, a 36% increase over the decade.[8] Of the patent applications filed at the Agency between 2007 and 2010, about 30% paid small entity filing fees (a discount available to individuals or businesses with fewer than 500 employees), even while by one measure more than 50% of all U.S. utility patent applications in both 2009 and 2010 originated from outside the United States.[9]

Although small businesses have originated approximately one-third of USPTO patent applications in recent years, too little data exists on how, why, or what share of U.S. small businesses are participating in the patent system. Some of the best evidence comes from a large scale survey—not of small businesses *per se*, but of startup businesses in their early years—conducted by researchers at the Ewing Marion Kauffman Foundation.[10] Using the most recent set of these data available, a picture of

---

[8] Patent Technology Monitoring Team, USPTO, *U.S. Patent Statistics Chart, Calendar Years 1963–2010, available at* http://www.uspto.gov/web/offices/ac/ido/oeip/taf/us_stat.htm.

[9] Analysis of USPTO data. This measure uses the nation of origin of the first named inventor on the application as an indicator of domestic and foreign origin.

[10] The Kauffman Firm Survey (KFS) is a data source derived from new businesses founded in 2004 and tracked each year, providing information on these businesses from startup to sustainability, with data across their early years focusing on subjects such as how businesses are financed; the products, services, and innovations these businesses

small entity patenting activity in the United States emerges. By employing stratification adjustments suggested by the Kauffman research team,[11] it is possible to develop a statistical representation of patenting by a cohort of U.S. small businesses founded in 2004 in their sixth year of operations.

These statistics show that holding patents by young startups in their sixth year of life is relatively uncommon. Analysis of the data demonstrates that only approximately 2.5 percent of these small-business respondents report any patenting activity, which can include filing applications, being granted patents, or purchasing patents from others. Among industries identified as "high technology," the share of companies with patenting activity is higher at approximately 8.0 percent, although only about 5.5 percent of all small businesses in the sample fall into the "high technology" category.[12]

2. Patenting can be important to the competitiveness of small businesses.

While these figures suggest that patenting is relatively uncommon among young small businesses, other evidence suggests that patenting is nevertheless important to high technology companies, and can be associated with superior economic performance. Because the initial cost associated with patent protection is relatively high for early startups, and because patents can have uncertain value, understanding the patenting-success relationship is relevant. Although academic economic research has not answered this question definitively, studies in both the United Kingdom and the United States have found that increased patenting is related to increased growth along several economically relevant dimensions.[13] Similarly, in a survey of young high-technology companies conducted in 2008, a group of researchers at the University of California, Berkeley found that patenting is quite common among biotechnology and medical device startups. When these companies had venture-capital funding, the share

---

possess and develop; and the characteristics of their owners and operators. Alicia Robb & E.J. Reedy, *An Overview of the Kauffman Firm Survey: Results from 2009 Business Activities* (Apr. 5, 2011), *available at* http://ssrn.com/abstract=1802597.

[11] *See generally* David DesRoches et al, *Kauffman Firm Survey Baseline Methodology Report* (Oct. 24, 2007) *available at* http://ssrn.com/abstract=1024045 (final report to the Ewing Marion Kauffman Foundation).

[12] Kauffman reports that the technology categories are based on the businesses' Standard Industry Classification (SIC) code designation, developed in the early 1990s by researchers at the Bureau of Labor Statistics. *See* Paul Hadlock et al, *High Technology Employment: Another View*, 114 MONTHLY LAB. REV. 26 (1991). The figures are consistent with the findings from earlier years of the survey, when these companies were younger. *See* Kauffman Foundation, *New Kauffman Foundation Study Offers Insights into the Earliest Years of a New Business* (March 12, 2008), *available at* http://www.kauffman.org/Details.aspx?id=1090.

[13] *See* Christian Helmers & Mark Rogers, *Does Patenting Help High-tech Start-ups?*, 40 RES. POL'Y 1016 (2011) (finding UK firms obtaining patents in the early 2000s to have significantly higher growth in total assets over the following five years), *and* Ronald J. Mann & Thomas W. Sager, *Patents, Venture Capital, and Software Start-ups*, 36 RES. POL'Y 193 (2007) (finding that U.S. venture-backed software firms holding patents in the late 1990s showed better later performance in venture capital financing based on total investment, how the firm exited, and how long the firm survived).

of companies engaged in patenting exceeded 90%.[14] Moreover, patenting was not uncommon even among information technology startups, including both software and internet companies.

Many high-tech startup executives stated that patenting was important for capturing competitive advantage in the marketplace, preventing copying, improving success at attracting investment, and increasing the likelihood of being acquired by another company or having a successful initial public offering (IPO). These last findings are supported by other economic researchers who have suggested a positive relationship between startup patenting, meaningful early investor funding, and successful transitions into larger publicly-traded firms.[15]

3. Internationalization strategies can facilitate small business growth and job creation.

In an increasingly global economy, internationalization strategies can be effective mechanisms to access markets, serve unmet demand, and grow small companies, thereby increasing manufacturing, production, and job creation. Various ways of entering non-domestic markets—such as licensing, franchising, exporting, and foreign direct investment—have been shown to be related to the growth and successful performance of small companies.[16] In addition, the U.S. government has recognized the importance of exporting to the economic health of the nation, and has taken action in the form of programs like the National Export Initiative (NEI).[17] The NEI also explicitly focuses on the importance of supporting exports by small and medium-sized enterprises.[18]

---

[14] *See* Stuart J.H. Graham et al, *High Technology Entrepreneurs and the Patent System: Results of the 2008 Berkeley Patent Survey*, 24 BERKELEY TECH. L.J. 255 (2009).

[15] Ronald J. Mann & Thomas W. Sager, *Patents, Venture Capital, and Software Start-ups*, 36 RES. POL'Y 193 (2007); David H. Hsu & Rosemarie H. Ziedonis, *Strategic Factor Markets and the Financing of Technology Startups: When Do Patents Matter More As Signaling Devices?* (June 2011), *available at* http://www-management.wharton.upenn.edu/hsu/inc/doc/papers/david-hsu-signaling.pdf. It is noteworthy that an inherent limitation of this kind of evidence, whether statistical or anecdotal, is that it is difficult to distinguish which way the causation runs. For instance, the growth, superior performance, and success of a small company may have been primarily the result of good managers, who also tend to select patenting because it is in their best interest to preserve the company's competitive options.

[16] *See, e.g.*, Joachim Wagner, *The Causal Effects of Exports on Firm Size and Labor Productivity: First Evidence from a Matching Approach*, 77 ECON. LETTERS 287 (2002), Jane W. Lul & Paul W. Beamish, *The Internationalization and Performance of SMEs*, 22 STRATEGIC MGMT. J. 565 (2001), *and* Antonio Majocchi & Antonella Zucchella, *Internationalization and Performance: Findings from a Set of Italian SMEs*, 21 INT'L SMALL BUS. J. 249 (2003).

[17] Exec. Order No. 13,534, 75 Fed. Reg. 12,433 (Mar. 11, 2010).

[18] Exec. Order No. 13,534, 75 Fed. Reg. 12,433 (Mar. 11, 2010).

4. Patent protection abroad opens opportunities for successful entry into global markets.

Economists recognize that a well-developed system of property rights, particularly for innovative companies, is often a precondition to successful internationalization.[19] The comments received in response to this study reflect a similar understanding among the IP and business community. For example, one respondent noted the importance for small- and medium-sized enterprises (SMEs):

> International patent protection is critical for SMEs that have inventions that are viable both in the domestic market and overseas. The international marketplace is extremely competitive as it is. American SMEs need every possible edge over their foreign competitors to secure on-going sales. Having patent protection for an advanced technology, or invention isn't a guarantee, but is a significant advantage.

From an economic perspective, patent rights can be thought of as options. While one must pursue patent protection today, the protection can have an extended life and thus provide future opportunities to engage in later productive economic activity.[20] One witness recognized this reality:

> A failure of SMEs with international strategies to obtain international patent protection early dramatically increases the risk that another business will beat them to the patent office and effectively block any possibility of growth in that country.[21]

These considerations also have technology- and industry-specific implications. One respondent from the electronic and software industry observed:

> The key reason [sic] that a small business needs patent protection outside the U.S. are those cases in which they wish to license another company to make and sell the product in countries outside the U.S. with the expectation that the product will never enter the U.S.[22]

Yet many small business owners are unaware that patent rights are territorial, and the protection offered by a U.S. patent ends at our borders.[23] Protection in other markets must be sought on a nation-by-nation basis. And many U.S. small businesses do not realize all the paths that they have at their disposal. One witness pointed to the lack of information among small businesses about acceleration mechanisms in international patent prosecution, such as work-sharing among patent offices and the Patent Prosecution Highway.[24]

---

[19] *See, e.g.*, Zoltan J. Acs et al, *The Internationalization of Small and Medium-Sized Enterprises: A Policy Perspective*, 9 SMALL BUS. ECON. 7 (1997).

[20] *See, e.g.*, Ariel Pakes, *Patents as Options: Some Estimates of the Value of Holding European Patent Stocks*, 54 ECONOMETRICA 755 (1986).

[21] Comments of American Intellectual Property Law Association, at 4, *available at* http://www.uspto.gov/aia_implementation/ipp-2011nov08-aipla.pdf.

[22] Comments of David Carlson, at 2, *available at* http://www.uspto.gov/aia_implementation/ipp-2011oct24-carlson-david.pdf.

[23] *See generally*, StopFakes.gov, http://www.uspto.gov/smallbusiness/about/faq.html (last visited Jan. 13, 2012).

[24] USC Hearing, at 32, available at http://www.uspto.gov/aia_implementation/111101-ipsb_transcript.pdf (Q&A with Christopher Palermo).

In order for a U.S. small business to maintain an option of selling or making its innovation in another country, it is often necessary to patent the innovation abroad. By doing so, a U.S. small business can prevent others from patenting the invention in those nations and prevent foreign competitors from simply copying the invention. Moreover, academic research has suggested that small business success in internationalization can be aided by partnering with larger companies with resources and expertise.[25] That may include collaborating with an established partner in the foreign market, which can require the possession of foreign patents. According to one witness:

> International partners will want to see local protection for their markets if they want to collaborate with the small company or invest/purchase. It is critical.[26]

The comments also noted the concentration of patenting in high-technology firms and discussed the relative scarcity in fact of patent-holding by young high technology firms. As to when small businesses should take an active interest in securing international patent protection, one respondent noted as follows:

> At the outset, international patent protection may be critical in the first few years of establishment. For startup high-tech businesses that have invented the core idea of a new technology, it is critical.[27]

Yet as to when small businesses actually do take an active interest in securing international patent protection, the same respondent also noted as follows:

> The small enterprise may realize that international patent protection is important, but it may not include that component in its business strategy until it is too late. Competitors in other countries may already have copied and used the invention, and even patented the same or similar inventions or their improvements, to the detriment of the original inventor.[28]

The comments in this regard were not uniform, however. Another respondent from the industrial equipment sector discussed the importance of international patenting not in terms of a company's high-technology focus, but rather of general marketability and foreign demand:

> International patent protection is crucial for SMEs whose inventions have [broad-based] appeal, are competitive and therefore have excellent export potential, versus those inventions that are limited in scope, or cannot compete on a cost [basis] with similar foreign inventions, and thus would be economically viable only in the U.S. domestic market.[29]

---

[25] *See, e.g.*, Zoltan J. Acs et al, *The Internationalization of Small and Medium-Sized Enterprises: A Policy Perspective*, 9 SMALL BUS. ECON. 7 (1997).

[26] Comments of Philip McGarrigle, at 4, *available at* http://www.uspto.gov/aia_implementation/ipp-2011nov01-mcgarrigle-philip.pdf.

[27] Comments of American Intellectual Property Law Association, at 3, *available at* http://www.uspto.gov/aia_implementation/ipp-2011nov08-aipla.pdf.

[28] Comments of American Intellectual Property Law Association, at 3, *available at* http://www.uspto.gov/aia_implementation/ipp-2011nov08-aipla.pdf.

[29] Comments of Power Clean 2000, Inc., at 1, *available at* http://www.uspto.gov/aia_implementation/ipp-2011nov09-power-clean-2000.pdf.

Other respondents suggested different reasons for international patenting, both those related to the reliability of enforcement and the availability of established partner firms in the pertinent foreign jurisdiction[30] and benefits associated with building markets and attracting investors.[31] Not least, one respondent specifically highlighted the absence of detailed empirical studies into what characteristics determine the importance of international patent protection for small businesses in different technology fields and in national markets of different size and distribution.[32]

5.   **Small businesses may be obtaining patent protection abroad less frequently than large companies.**

In 1995, the U.S. Small Business Administration (SBA) commissioned a statistical study that found U.S. small businesses possessing U.S. patents issued in 1988 were less likely than their large counterparts to extend their patent protection to other countries.[33] This study used metrics suggesting that the difference could not be explained by small businesses producing less valuable or less important inventions, or engaging in technologies where patenting or foreign business was considered less important. Nevertheless, though the SBA report suggested that the lower rate of foreign patenting among small businesses was not driven by lower-value innovation or industry effects, the report's findings were not conclusive.

A follow-on report commissioned by the SBA and released in 2003 used statistical analysis to examine U.S. patents granted to U.S. small businesses during 1988, 1992, 1996, and 1998.[34] By comparing these patents to those held by large companies, the report found that small businesses were extending their patent protection outside the U.S. less frequently than large entities irrespective of technology field, suggesting that the differences were not a product of these companies working in different industry sectors.

Neither of these SBA reports, however, discussed whether the differences in foreign patenting behavior had any relationship to the success of these companies, or their performance in terms of growth, employment, sales, or profits. Also, there was no evidence presented that larger companies extended

---

[30] Comments of Power Clean 2000, Inc., at 1, *available at* http://www.uspto.gov/aia_implementation/ipp-2011nov09-power-clean-2000.pdf.

[31] Comments of David Carlson, at 1, *available at* http://www.uspto.gov/aia_implementation/ipp-2011oct24-carlson-david.pdf.

[32] Testimony of Dr. Jay Kesan, at 2, *available at* http://www.uspto.gov/aia_implementation/ipp-2011oct31-kesan-jay.pdf.

[33] Mogee Research & Analysis Associates, *Foreign Patenting Behavior of Small and Large Firms*, Final Report to the Small Business Administration under Contract No. SBA-8140 (1996), *available at* http://archive.sba.gov/advo/research/rs167.html.

[34] Mary Ellen Mogee, *Foreign Patenting Behavior of Small and Large Firms: An Update*, Report to the Small Business Administration under Contract No. SBAHQ-01-M-0357 (2003), *available at* http://archive.sba.gov/advo/research/rs228_tot.pdf.

protection abroad at the optimal level, or that small businesses, by comparison, extended protection to a sub-optimal degree.

Commentary at the hearings discussed these issues. One respondent spoke of the competing interests in the early life of the company, and why international patenting may happen less frequently at small and medium-sized enterprises (SMEs):

> SMEs also tend to see foreign patents as a low priority benefit in the early stages of the business. Priorities are finalizing product design, marketing and sales to result in "winning" in the marketplace, and obtaining a U.S. patent position if appropriate.[35]

Indeed, another of the comments suggests that this difference is driven largely by the high cost of obtaining patent protection internationally. According to one witness:

> International patents are expensive, and small businesses have other competing priorities for their capital. . . . With regard to the acquisition of international patent rights, translation costs, annuity fees, and foreign professional fees represent significant expenses and act as barriers that often prevent small businesses from applying for foreign patents.[36]

The problem of high cost in international patenting is further complicated by the limited time in which to decide where to pursue national stage patent protection spun off from a Patent Cooperation Treaty application:

> For example, a biotech company that files a U.S. patent application today (and a PCT application one year from now) has only 30 months to decide whether to abandon the application if it wants to avoid the cost of entering the national stage in a number of foreign countries. 30 months may be enough in some other industries, but in biotech that's too soon for an informed decision. Including translation costs, the aggregate expense of entering the national stage in Japan, Korea, Europe, Australia, and the NAFTA countries can easily exceed $100,000; if the BRIC countries are added, costs can double.[37]

Moreover, U.S. small businesses perceive working capital to be even more important in light of the first-to-file provision of the AIA:

> And this need for cash comes even earlier under the America Invents Act. Since the U.S. will be a first to file country, U.S. filings will come as soon as possible and the foreign filing decisions will be stepped up. Moving expenses up for an early stage small life science company is more difficult and the probability increases that these early inventions are not adequately protected.

---

[35] Comments of Christopher Palermo, at 1, *available at* http://www.uspto.gov/aia_implementation/ipp-2011nov01-palermo-christopher.pdf.

[36] Comments of American Intellectual Property Law Association, at 3, 5, *available at* http://www.uspto.gov/aia_implementation/ipp-2011nov08-aipla.pdf.

[37] Comments of Biotechnology Industry Association, at 3, *available at* http://www.uspto.gov/aia_implementation/ipp-2011oct20-bio.pdf.

Small companies usually do not have much available cash which makes paying foreign filing expenses more difficult. They run leanly and need to periodically raise capital to fund their operations. However, they do not raise more money than necessary in the short term it would require selling too much equity at a low price.[38]

Nor does the high importance of international patent protection appear to depend on technology field, according to one respondent:

International protection is critical for any small business that develops a new drug or medical device, since there may be no other clinically acceptable alternative. A patent on that new drug or device will ensure exclusivity for an extended period of the drug or device's market lifetime. In the wireless and IT sectors, if a small business does not have patents in as many countries as possible and as soon as possible, it may be very difficult to obtain local investment in its venture.[39]

Indeed, the relative importance of international patent protection may, to an extent, be altogether unknowable for many firms early in their development. Patenting abroad becomes significant, according to one respondent,

usually 3-6 years after the invention has been made at the earliest, more often, 10 years after the invention has been made. When a small business is starting, they cannot predict very with much accuracy where the market for the product will develop, who the primary buyers will be across the globe and the time it will take to move a product from the idea stage to the market stage.[40]

Moreover, most small firms plan to patent internationally based not on their own manufacturing or marketing operations, but rather on an established, licensed partner firm:

In the context of a small business, they do not expect to be selling product in many countries; if they did, they would be a large company. Nearly all small businesses do not have the production and market distribution capability to sell internationally themselves. Rather, they will achieve this by licensing an established company who has such . . . distribution chains available. The other company might be a large U.S. company, a large company in another country or a very large multi-national company.[41]

The USPTO public hearing in October revealed an illustrative pair of case studies on the importance of foreign patenting to the success of a small business. The first firm dealt in traffic surveillance technology. The second firm dealt in imaging technology.

---

[38] Comments of Philip McGarrigle, at 2, *available at* http://www.uspto.gov/aia_implementation/ipp-2011nov01-mcgarrigle-philip.pdf.

[39] Comments of American Intellectual Property Law Association, at 4, *available at* http://www.uspto.gov/aia_implementation/ipp-2011nov08-aipla.pdf.

[40] Comments of David Carlson, at 1, *available at* http://www.uspto.gov/aia_implementation/ipp-2011oct24-carlson-david.pdf.

[41] Comments of David Carlson, at 1, *available at* http://www.uspto.gov/aia_implementation/ipp-2011oct24-carlson-david.pdf.

a.   Case Study: Traffic Surveillance Technology

In studying Washington, DC, traffic patterns, a group of professors at the University of Maryland recognized that most modern car keys employ short-range wireless transmitter technology such as Bluetooth®.[42] By detecting each key's wireless identifier as cars pass by, it is possible to determine how many cars are on the road and how fast each is going, all in real time without the need for cameras. Extensive research and development went into using this technology to manage traffic through existing infrastructure.

The professors then turned to business strategy. They obtained patents on their invention and formed a company with support from the university to commercialize their invention. They obtained venture capital funding and invested in competent personnel. And they sought clients, expecting first to establish their brand in the greater Washington, DC, area, which is known for its severe traffic congestion problems. Yet their first business came in foreign markets, including Singapore and Sweden.

The firm took a far-sighted approach and pursued international patent protection, including the substantial cost of foreign translation. The firm did so at a time when it had limited capital. Because the firm invested in protecting its promising technology in multiple foreign markets, it has now built an internationally successful brand that cannot easily be copied by foreign rivals. And where the firm wishes to deploy its traffic surveillance technology through other companies who can better meet local demands, it is strongly positioned to capture licensing revenues.

b.   Case Study: Scanning and Imaging Technology

A small American imaging firm operated in the market for scanners.[43] The owner had previously been an employee at Kodak and had a sophisticated understanding of imaging technology. The firm's scanner products commanded quite high prices in the market, upwards of $10,000 per unit, as the scanners themselves reflected the state of the art. Not surprisingly, a great deal of patented technology and software went into developing and producing the firm's scanners.

The firm's owner, however, met with its intellectual property counsel and learned that acquiring international patent protection, particularly through the PCT process and in light of the translations required for multiple foreign jurisdictions, was procedurally complex and quite expensive. Therefore, management made the business decision to obtain patents only in the United States and in Australia, but not, for example, in Europe, Japan, or China—major trading partners of the United States.

---

[42] *See* USPTO Hearing, at 21–24, *available at* http://www.uspto.gov/aia_implementation/111027-ipsb_transcript.pdf.
[43] *See* USPTO Hearing, at 24–26, *available at* http://www.uspto.gov/aia_implementation/111027-ipsb_transcript.pdf.

Soon after, at an industry conference in Germany, the owner discovered that a German firm was demonstrating scanner products that used the very same core technology that he had pioneered. The German company was well-funded and successful, and was quite candid that it had derived its products from the American inventor and his small business. Yet the German firm highlighted its considerable corporate backing and network of clients and existing service agreements, and carried away a great deal of business as a result.

The American inventor consulted his intellectual property counsel regarding the situation in Germany, but learned that he was bound by his earlier economic decision to abdicate patent protection in most foreign countries. Unless the German firm imported its scanners into the U.S., disputing the expropriation was, ironically, not worth the option.

Later, testifying before Congress on this issue, the American small business owner lamented that his intention had never been to drive the German firm out of the market. To the contrary, he would have preferred to do business with them: grant them a license and mutually enjoy the benefit of their resources and distribution networks. Only his early and difficult economic choice left him with no bargaining position. He had unwittingly made a royalty-free donation to an overseas competitor only too grateful to capture the market and the jobs, without taking the risk or expending resources on research and development.

6.   International patenting costs are often substantial.

In comparison to the United States, patenting in other international markets tends to be expensive. It may be impossible to compare the entirety of economic costs and benefits of patenting in one nation versus another due to differences in patent scope, patent laws, and patent enforcement. Nevertheless, it is possible at least to compare the levels of patent-office fees faced by a typical small entity seeking patent protection in different countries.

Significantly, the U.S. recognizes applicants who qualify for "small entity" status and provides a 50% fee discount to such entities and, under new law, a 75% discount to a "micro entity."[44] By comparison, those patent offices around the world which U.S. companies principally target for international protection tend to charge much higher fees.[45] Foreign patent offices also tend to be

---

[44] As of 2011, the USPTO charges three preliminary fees to small entities: a $95 filing fee, $310 search fee, $125 examination fee (totaling $530). A small business is required to pay another fee of $875 fee at patent issue. The USPTO also requires that, in order to keep the patent in force, the patentee must pay post-grant maintenance fees at staggered intervals, equaling $565 at 3½ years from issuance, $1,425 at 7½ years from issuance, and $2,365 at 11½ years from issuance. *See* USPTO Fee Schedule, http://www.uspto.gov/curr_fees (last visited Jan. 13, 2012). Moreover, the AIA mandates reduced fees for micro-entities. *See* Pub. L. No. 112-29, § 10(b).

[45] As a comparison point, the following calculations are based on a patent application in several countries containing 23 claims (allowing a comparison to the USPTO basic filing fee which allows 3 independent claims and 20

substantially more expensive for U.S. small businesses because of the undiscounted annual maintenance fees charged.[46]

While there are substantial differences in the fees paid to patent offices to secure and maintain a patent, such fees only represent a fraction of the total costs of patenting paid by small businesses. Small businesses pay patent attorneys for their services and for required language translations. Translation is expensive in general, and technical translation significantly more so. Recent economic research suggests that required translations into the national languages needed in many international patent offices can be a significant disincentive for companies to seek patent protection in these other countries.[47] Including translation costs, the General Accounting Office in 2003 estimated a cost of between $160,000-320,000 in foreign patenting costs to a U.S. company seeking protection in four foreign jurisdictions (Japan, Canada, South Korea, and the European Patent Office). Such costs will necessarily depend on which countries are chosen and the complexity of the invention.

The IP community has specifically noted the disparity. One witness discussed it in terms of the

---

dependent claims). The following calculations compare fees paid for such a typical application at the USPTO with fees that would be paid by a U.S. small business at the European Patent Office (EPO), the Japan Patent Office (JPO), and the China State Intellectual Property Office (SIPO).

At the European Patent Office (EPO), for instance, preliminary fees for applicants include a €105 filing fee ($134 in 2010), a €1105 search fee that includes Europe ($1,510 in 2010), a €1785 international search fee ($2274 in 2010), and a €1480 examination fee ($1,885 in 2010), totaling a 2010 equivalent of $5803, more than ten times the equivalent cost for similar services for small businesses in the USPTO. *See* European (EPC) Fees, http://www.epo.org/applying/forms-fees/fees.html (last visited Jan. 13, 2012).

The JPO charges a ¥24,000 filing fee ($262 in 2010), and an examination fee of ¥118,000 ($1,292 in 2010) plus ¥4,000 per patent claim ($44 in 2010), which in the stylized example of 23 claims would equal a 2010 U.S. dollar equivalent of $2,561 for all these preliminary costs, about five times more expensive than these services offered to small entities at the USPTO. *See* JPO Schedule of Fees, http://www.jpo.go.jp/tetuzuki_e/ryoukin_e/ryokine.htm (last visited Jan. 13, 2012).

[46] As a comparison point, the following calculations are based on a patent application in several countries containing 23 claims (allowing a comparison to the USPTO basic filing fee which allows 3 independent claims and 20 dependent claims).

The EPO requires annual fees, so-called annuities, both during the application phase and after a patent is allowed. These fees amount to €420 a year beginning at year three, €525 at year four, €735 at year five, €945 at year six, €1,050 at year seven, €1,155 at year eight, €1,260 at year nine, and €1,420 at years ten and greater. *See* European (EPC) Fees, http://www.epo.org/applying/forms-fees/fees html (last visited Jan. 13, 2012).

At the JPO, annual renewal fees are ¥2,300 plus ¥200 per claim for years 1–3, ¥7,100 plus ¥500 per claim for years 4–6, ¥21,400 plus ¥1,700 per claim for years 7–9, and ¥61,600 plus ¥4,800 per claim for year 10 and greater. *See* JPO Schedule of Fees, http://www.jpo.go.jp/tetuzuki e/ryoukin e/ryokine htm (last visited Jan. 13, 2012).

Similarly, the Chinese SIPO requires annual maintenance fees of RMB1,200 per year for years 4–6, RMB2,000 per year for years 7–9, RMB4,000 per year for years 10–12, RMB6,000 per year for years 13–15, and RMB8,000 per year for year 16 and thereafter. *See* Schedule of Fees for Chinese Patent (All-China Patent Agents Association), http://www.liu-shen.com/docs/SFBEN.pdf (last visited Jan. 13, 2012).

[47] Dietmar Harhoff et al, *Languages, Fees and the International Scope of Patenting* (Centre for Econ. Pol'y Res., Discussion Paper No. 7241, 2009), *available at* http://www2.druid.dk/conferences/viewpaper.php?id=5704&cf=32.

broader problem of cost to small businesses. A first cost is official fees:

> The overall official fees for filing are higher in most foreign jurisdictions than in the US, and there are no small entity discounts. Excess claims fees are particularly high in the EPO.[48]

A second is translation costs:

> The cost of the lawyer is actually less than the cost of the translation in certain cases. So what you would think, the highly trained, really valuable patent lawyer guy that says, that's going to cost me a fortune, but when I add up my translation cost, that actually flips the equation, I am spending more to get the translation than I am on the attorney.[49]

A third is the cost of outside counsel, both in the U.S. and abroad.

> SME discounts are rare overseas, if available at all. Fixed costs and hourly rates for attorneys in, say, London or Tokyo are perceived to be significantly higher than those of their U.S. counterparts. Foreign firms do not have the kind of SME-serving culture that exists in, say, the California bar.[50]

Furthermore, in comparison to the United States, the process to secure a foreign patent can be overwhelming. A separate application is generally required in each country in which protection is sought. There are two international procedures that can be useful in obtaining protection. One, established under the Paris Convention, allows an ordinary application to be filed in each foreign country in which protection is desired, within one year of when the application is filed in the United States (or other first country). The second method, the Patent Cooperation Treaty (PCT), must also be pursued within a year of original filing; it allows for a form of international patent search to be carried out, but there remains substantive and administrative processing needed for each treaty-member country in which protection is desired, plus the payment of fees and other costs. One advantage to using the PCT route for the applicant is that it allows one to defer these various "national-phase" examinations for at least 30 months after the original filing.

Comments reflected that the PCT method can be a useful one for a small business, with one witness noting that the PCT "is the preeminent vehicle for pursuing international patent protection."[51] The USPTO also received testimony from a practitioner whose twenty years of experience has included "substantial use of PCT practice."[52] The witness explained the benefit of using the PCT system:

---

[48] Comments of Christopher Palermo, at 1, *available at* http://www.uspto.gov/aia_implementation/ipp-2011nov01-palermo-christopher.pdf.

[49] USPTO Hearing, at 28 (testimony of Morgan Reed), *available at* http://www.uspto.gov/aia_implementation/111027-ipsb_transcript.pdf.

[50] Comments of Christopher Palermo, at 2, *available at* http://www.uspto.gov/aia_implementation/ipp-2011nov01-palermo-christopher.pdf.

[51] Comments of American Intellectual Property Law Association, at 2, *available at* http://www.uspto.gov/aia_implementation/ipp-2011nov08-aipla.pdf.

[52] USPTO Hearing, at 52 (testimony of Timothy King), *available at* http://www.uspto.gov/aia_implementation/111027-ipsb_transcript.pdf.

> I can count on . . . one hand the number of times where I've gone direct national rather than using the PCT system. So I think qualitatively it's done a very good job to facilitate the winnowing out of cases that are weaker than others.[53]

Yet the same witness also qualified his regard for the PCT:

> But I think the critical limitation with respect to the PCT system in general is that you have to file 12 months before you have all the information that you garner from the PCT process. And so if you have information available to you at the time of foreign filing or entering the process, you will be able to make much better business decisions about those patents that you would proceed with.[54]

Beyond procedural limitations, moreover, some comments about the PCT also identified drawbacks to using the system. One respondent framed the issue as one of fee deferral:

> [Most startups] also view PCT solely as a fee deferral system, mainly because the International Search Reports prepared for their technologies do not result in useful information, and because examining standards for IT-related subject matter differ greatly around the world, making centralized amendments is not particularly useful.[55]

7. Patenting expenses often occur early in the life of small businesses and are difficult to fund.

Because small businesses are often cash-constrained, the amount of capital and funding they possess can be an important limitation on their ability to obtain patent protection. An early-stage startup may be pursuing patent applications, both in the U.S. and abroad, at the same time as it is seeking and obtaining funding and making other early-stage investments in equipment, development, and hiring employees. Often, the point at which capital is necessary for investing in patent protection—which must be expended early in the development of a new innovation due to patent priority rules—will require that the company forego other investments in its future growth and success. This suggests that uncertainty about technical and commercial potential of the business plays a huge role, and the relationship between the initial funding cycle for young companies and the initial patent lifecycle is an important consideration.

While small business owners often use personal funds, credit, and cash flows from operations to fund growth, many also seek funding from external sources. They may obtain loans from commercial lenders or equity investments from friends and family, so-called "angel" investors, or venture-capital firms, among other sources. Many startup companies fail, and the survivors are often cash-constrained for a number of years in their early lives.[56] A small number of startups will develop into "gazelles," fast

---

[53] USPTO Hearing, at 52–53 (testimony of Timothy King), *available at* http://www.uspto.gov/aia_implementation/111027-ipsb_transcript.pdf.

[54] USPTO Hearing, at 53 (testimony of Timothy King), *available at* http://www.uspto.gov/aia_implementation/111027-ipsb_transcript.pdf.

[55] Comments of Christopher Palermo, at 1, *available at* http://www.uspto.gov/aia_implementation/ipp-2011nov01-palermo-christopher.pdf.

[56] *See generally* Paul A. Gompers & Joshua Lerner, THE VENTURE CAPITAL CYCLE (2004).

19

growing companies between 3 and 5 years of age. A recent economic study suggests that these "gazelles" account for less than 1 percent of all U.S. companies yet generate about 10% of new jobs per year.[57] This same research finds that throughout the American economy in recent years, just 1% of companies, the top performers, contributed as much as 40% of the total employment growth, and these top performers are heavily concentrated in companies of less than 500 employees.[58]

The extension of patent protection during the last several decades to include software and business methods has increased the pool of U.S. small businesses that may seek patent protection for their innovations. When an innovating company seeks patent protection, it faces a sequence of costs that must be paid to patent offices (in fees) and to patent practitioners (for preparing documents) at a time when the typical startup company is cash-constrained. Thus, small businesses may select against patenting early in life and face later, negative ramifications. According to one witness familiar with the information technology (IT) industry:

> Venture capitalists and other early-stage investors in IT businesses tend to view patent exclusivity as a secondary factor because the real problem is competing in the market against established behemoths on the merits of product features and functions. Patents become more important in years 3 and later when the future of the business is more apparent, second-tier investors have entered or a revenue stream exists.[59]

On top of what may be large expenditures for research and development by the small company, the total cost to obtain even U.S. patent protection can average almost $40 thousand dollars,[60] and increase considerably depending on the complexity of the invention and on prosecution options such as appeals and interferences.[61] These costs may be multiplied many times over if the small business seeks to extend its patent protection in other nations.[62]

The timing of international patenting costs is important when compared to the funding timeline of the typical early-stage company. Up-front patenting costs are significant, with a large portion coming in the form of attorney costs and translation fees. At the earliest point in a young company's life, cash flows tend to be the most limited and constrained. Often, early-stage companies have negative cash-flow, so any

---

[57] Dane Stangler, *High-Growth Firms and the Future of the American Economy*, March 2010 (Kauffman Foundation)

[58] The U.S. government currently offers financial support through myriad programs to small businesses. For instance, the 2011 launch of the Startup America program included several initiatives including the SBA-led launch of two $1 billion initiatives for impact investing and early-stage seed financing. *See* Startup America: Obama Administration Commitments, http://www.whitehouse.gov/issues/startup-america-public (last visited Jan. 13, 2012).

[59] Comments of Christopher Palermo, at 1, *available at* http://www.uspto.gov/aia_implementation/ipp-2011nov01-palermo-christopher.pdf.

[60] *See* Stuart J.H. Graham et al, *High Technology Entrepreneurs and the Patent System: Results of the 2008 Berkeley Patent Survey*, 24 BERKELEY TECH. L.J. 255 (2009).

[61] *See, e.g.*, AMERICAN INTELLECTUAL PROPERTY LAW ASSOCIATION, 2011 REPORT OF THE ECONOMIC SURVEY (2011).

[62] *See, e.g.*, Anne M. Scheiderman, "Filing International Patent Applications under the Patent Cooperation Treaty (PCT): Strategies for Delaying Costs and Maximizing the Value of Your Intellectual Property Worldwide" *in* IPHANDBOOK OF BEST PRACTICES § 10.7, *available at* http://www.iphandbook.org/handbook/ch10/p07/.

investment in patenting must either come from personal funds, debt, investor capital, or be foregone altogether.

In addition, the returns to patenting may be uncertain. A substantial body of economic literature shows that the value distribution in patenting is highly skewed, with only a relatively small fraction of patents producing large financial returns to the patentee.[63] Unfortunately, patenting is required to be initiated at the beginning of the innovation process, when uncertainty over the technological potential of the invention, and its commercial potential in the marketplace, tends to be high. Therefore, small businesses must often make patent-protection investments early during a situation of high uncertainty, while not fully able to predict how meaningful the patent protection may be to the company's future competitiveness. Such uncertainty may result in a small business either under-investing or over-investing in patent protection in these early stages.

Under normal circumstances, information about a company's prospects should become apparent over time as the business tests market demand. When markets for entrepreneurial capital are operating reasonably efficiently, investors should be willing to put capital into businesses that appear to be good investment candidates. So over time, capital should be available to these companies so long as they are better able to demonstrate the commercial potential of their inventions. Under such circumstances, successful small businesses ought to be better able to bear costs that occur as the company grows and later in the patenting life cycle. Because later patenting expenditures, such as renewal fees and enforcement costs, generally occur many years after the initial patent application filing phase, there may be less reason to believe that the markets for entrepreneurial capital are failing systematically many years after the founding of companies.

Many of the comments and testimony supported this concept. In several instances, witnesses observed that public support for expenditures later in the international patent protection process is not optimal, tending to disfavor later-stage funding assistance on a number of scores. Industry representatives suggested that late-stage funding is normatively inappropriate for activities such as maintenance:

> The start-up business that has found the money to remain in business for five to ten years when most maintenance expenses are first due should use its own money to maintain its patent rights. AIPLA does not believe that there is a role for the USPTO or other federal agencies in such activity.[64]

Another witness posited that late-stage funding is not undersupplied in activities such as enforcement, particularly because by then the patent information tends to be better developed (but not always):

---

[63] *See generally* Jean O. Lanjouw et al, *How to Count Patents and Value Intellectual Property: The Uses of Patent Renewal and Application Data*, 46 J. INDUS. ECON. 405 (1996).
[64] USPTO Hearing, at 65 (testimony of Alan Kasper), *available at* http://www.uspto.gov/aia_implementation/111027-ipsb_transcript.pdf.

With regard to enforcing international patent rights, I think much of the focus today has been on the procurement side, and certainly that's where the expenditures are most acute because the technology is not yet proven, so it's an investment.

On the enforcement side, generally speaking, for two parties to have a dispute, there is already [a] value proposition associated with the patent. So I think the issues, in my opinion, at least, are less acute; however, if you get to the stage of enforcement, if you find your patent is not worth what you thought, that clearly is a problem.[65]

Another witness echoed this view of late-stage funding as simply less important than early assistance for filing and prosecuting patents:

QUESTION: Given limited funds, whether it's a loan program or a grant program or if there are funds available, when are those funds most important? In the front end, filing, or what the legislation also envisions as maintenance? When is it more important?

WITNESS: I think it's unquestionable that it's front end, because if I'm going to be successful, somebody is going to give me money for maintenance.[66]

8. Foreign countries largely take a different approach than the United States in assisting small businesses to acquire patent protection.

Since 1982, the U.S. government has chosen to support patenting by small entities by discounting USPTO fees by 50 percent for independent inventors, small businesses, and non-profit organizations through a "small entity" status designation.[67] Congress originally enacted the small entity discount to alleviate the burden of 1982 increases in patent filing, processing, maintenance, and issue fees.[68] At the time, maintenance fees themselves had only recently been instituted, in 1980.[69] Significantly, the fees charged and fee discounts offered by the USPTO apply to both U.S. applicants and foreign applicants.

The motivation for these benefits is an appreciation by Congress that independent inventors, small businesses, and non-profit organizations seeking patent protection for their innovations should not bear the same economic burdens as well-established firms and corporations.[70] Indeed, the AIA goes further, adding a seventy-five percent discount for smaller "micro entities."[71]

---

[65] USPTO Hearing, at 98–99 (testimony of Steven Caltrider) , *available at* http://www.uspto.gov/aia_implementation/111027-ipsb_transcript.pdf.

[66] USPTO Hearing, at 35 (Q&A with Morgan Reed) , *available at* http://www.uspto.gov/aia_implementation/111027-ipsb_transcript.pdf.

[67] Act of Aug. 27, 1982, Pub. L. No. 97–247, § 1, 96 Stat. 317 (1982), *implemented by* 47 Fed. Reg. 40,134, 40, 139–40 (codified as amended, at 37 C.F.R. §§ 1.27, 1.28 (1983)).

[68] *Ulead Sys., Inc. v. Lex Computer & Mgmt. Corp.*, 351 F.3d 1139, 1142 (Fed. Cir. 2003).

[69] Act of Dec. 12, 1980, Pub. L. No. 96–517, § 2, 94 Stat. 3015, 3017–18 (1980).

[70] H. Rept. 112–98 (report of the House Committee on the Judiciary), *available at* http://www.gpo.gov/fdsys/pkg/CRPT-112hrpt98/pdf/CRPT-112hrpt98-pt1.pdf.

[71] A "micro-entity" is defined in pertinent part as an entity or person who has not been named as an inventor or more than 4 previously filed U.S. non-provisional patent applications and whose income does not exceed 3 times the U.S. median household income. Leahy-Smith America Invents Act, Pub. L. No. 112–29, §§ 10(b), 10(g) (2011).

The large majority of countries do not accommodate small entities in the same nondiscriminatory manner. Canada and Mexico are notable exceptions. Canada offers a 50 percent discount to entities that employ 50 or fewer employees or are universities,[72] while Mexico offers a 50 percent discount in filing fees to domestic or foreign individuals, independent inventors, small business concerns, and non-profit institutions.[73]

Beyond these, Japan and South Korea provide certain accommodations, but these incentives are not available to foreign applicants on an equal basis with domestic applicants. Japan recognizes small entity status for applicants who are supported according to the Daily Life Security Act; who are Japanese individuals not subject to a residency tax or an income tax; who are companies with capital less than 300m yen, are not subject to a corporation tax, and are not controlled by any other corporation; or who are national universities, national technical colleges, university-cooperative organizations, or small- or medium-sized R&D enterprises. Where the applicant is also the inventor, the individual applicant in the Korean Intellectual Property Office may receive up to a 70% reduction in fees, but otherwise small entities from other countries are not eligible for discounted fees. The European Patent Office and the State Intellectual Property Office of China do not offer any small entity discounts at all.

In contrast to the U.S.-led policy of neutrally applied fee discounts and impartiality as to technology sector or the national origin of applicants, a number of countries have pursued a policy of direct subsidization. China may be the most notable example. In 2006, China's *Outline of National Medium- and Long-Term Science and Technology Development Plan (2006-2020)* announced a new "innovation strategy" to the international community with the goal of "advancing China into the rank of innovative countries by 2020."[74] These initiatives included intent to invest more than 2.5% GDP in R&D, reduce dependence on foreign technology by 30%, and dramatically increase the number of annually granted "indigenous invention" patents.

Since then, China has made concerted efforts to broaden its intellectual property system[75] and increase both domestic and international patent filings. Direct government subsidization of Chinese citizens' patent applications and maintenance fees has been a particularly notable mechanism for supporting this increase. Chinese government subsidization of patenting can occur through two different channels, including (1) direct subsidization by the State Intellectual Property Office of the People's

---

[72] Patent Rules of Canada, SOR/96-423 § 3.01(3), *available at* http://laws-lois.justice.gc.ca/eng/regulations/SOR-96-423/index.html. Furthermore, small entities cannot be controlled by any entity that employs more than 50 employees and is not a university, and cannot be under an obligation of assignment or license in the invention to such an entity.
[73] *See* http://www2.aipla.org/html/patent-handbook/countries/mexico/MXgeneral html.
[74] Wu Zhongze, Vice Minister of Science and Technology, People's Republic of China, Innovation: China's New National Strategy, Address at the Opening Ceremony of China-EU Science and Technology Year (Oct. 11, 2006), *available at* http://ec.europa.eu/research/iscp/eu-china/pdf/vm_wu_speech_en.pdf.
[75] State Intellectual Property Office, People's Republic of China, National Patent Development Strategy (2011–2020), *available at* http://graphics8 nytimes.com/packages/pdf/business/SIPONatPatentDevStrategy.pdf.

Republic of China (SIPO), and (2) local government subsidization for patent applications and maintenance.[76] The importance of these subsidies to meeting the patent filing goals is clearly spelled out in SIPO's "*Guidance Regulations on subsidization work of patent application*," which asserts that subsidization promotes patenting of innovative ideas, and improves native technological innovation. Additionally, the increased emphasis on subsidized patent support (at lower monetary levels for applications and higher ones for successful grants)[77] can be seen through such examples as:

(a)   Beijing municipal government's 2006 stated intention of awarding citizens RMB 1,000 for patents applied for in foreign countries ("*Reward Measures on Patent Application in Beijing*"); and

(b)   Tianjin municipal government's 2006 stated intention of awarding citizen's RMB 5,000 for patents granted in other countries ("*Subsidization Measures of Patent Fees in Tianjin*").

Many provinces have also amplified their subsidization level per patent in recent years. For example, Zhejiang province's local subsidization amount rose from an initial 2,000 RMB per patent to 4,000 RMB in 2006. This may be due to variety of factors, but establishment of patent growth targets within some local governments (e.g. desired 30% annual growth in Anhui province in 2007) likely contributed to augmentation of local subsidization. At the same time, there is no evidence that such subsidies or patenting targets have increased either innovation or economic growth.

Other structural policies also greatly contribute to an increase in patenting. These include such items as mandatory "Inventor Remuneration" (Articles 16) and mandated first filing in China for inventions created there (Article 20) from the Third Amendment to China's Patent Law (2009).[78]

9.   **In response to the questions presented by Congress, the USPTO has identified points of agreement among respondents and witnesses as to what the U.S. Government can do to help small businesses with international patent protection.**

An overwhelming majority of respondents proposed that the United States work with foreign governments to reduce the costs associated with filing patent applications overseas and to harmonize legal requirements, particularly through existing treaty arrangements.

---

[76] Wen Jainchun et al, *Research on Patent Fees Subsided by Local Government in China*, in PROC. INT'L CONF. ON INFO. MGMT., INNOVATION MGMT. & INDUS. ENGINEERING (2008), *available at* http://ieeexplore.ieee.org/stamp/stamp.jsp?tp=&arnumber=4737773.

[77]Zhen Lei et al, Patent Subsidy and Patent Filing in China, Address at the Conference on Innovation and Patent Harmonization (Sept. 30–Oct. 1, 2011).

[78] Jason Cooper & Stephanie Chu, SURGE IN CHINESE INNOVATION AND THE IP IMPLICATIONS (2009), *available at* http://www.ipo.org/AM/Template.cfm?Section=Patents&Template=/CM/ContentDisplay.cfm&ContentID=28247.

a. The U.S. Government should engage in diplomacy and harmonization to reduce the costs associated with filing foreign patent applications.

With respect to reducing foreign patenting costs through diplomacy and harmonization, one industry organization reported as follows:

> With regard to the acquisition of international patent rights, translation costs, annuity fees, and foreign professional fees represent significant expenses and act as barriers that often prevent small businesses from applying for foreign patents. The USPTO and Federal Government could work with foreign governments to delay the requirement for submitting a translation, especially in countries with deferred examination. They also could work to reduce annuity payments for small enterprises during the pendency of an application.[79]

A manufacturing firm reported as follows:

> If possible, help negotiate down the cost of filing for small inventors. The initial filing costs for patents are daunting. The fees vary by economy and routinely range from hundreds to thousands of dollars per filing. This does not include the mandatory annual maintenance fees and continuous legal fees related to the prosecution of the application, which could take years to complete. There are a number of major markets that are not part of the PCT. Even with a PCT filing, the application still needs to be filed and prosecuted individually in each member economy. As a result, many SMEs do not file for patent protection in markets outside of the US, because they simply cannot afford to.[80]

With an academic perspective, one practitioner-turned-law professor reported as follows:

> Reduction in filing fees for small businesses for PCT applications would help significantly. In particular, if the PCT application filing fee is lowered to a level equivalent to or less than the typical search fee charged by a search firm for a patentability search, then it is well worthwhile for small businesses to file a PCT because they can obtain patentability search results from the PCT prior art search.
>
> Even if the overall fee associated with a PCT application cannot be reduced, the PTO should consider reducing at least the PCT search fee. It is not uncommon nowadays for patent counsel to suggest to their clients that they go and get their PCT search done in Korea instead of the U.S. because a search in Korea costs about half as much as a U.S. PCT search (about $1000 in Korea compared to about $2000 in the U.S.).[81]

A manufacturing firm reported as follows:[82]

> There is a complete lack of harmonization in the foreign patent application process. In fact, a patent could be granted in one economy, yet rejected in another. This uncertainty

---

[79] Comments of American Intellectual Property Law Association, at 6, *available at* http://www.uspto.gov/aia_implementation/ipp-2011nov08-aipla.pdf.

[80] Comments of Power Clean 2000, at 2, *available at* http://www.uspto.gov/aia_implementation/ipp-2011nov09-power-clean-2000.pdf.

[81] Comments of Jay Kesan, at 3–4, *available at* http://www.uspto.gov/aia_implementation/ipp-2011oct31-kesan-jay.pdf.

[82] Comments of Power Clean 2000, at 2, *available at* http://www.uspto.gov/aia_implementation/ipp-2011nov09-power-clean-2000.pdf.

is extremely frustrating for SMEs. And, unlike large companies with full legal departments, SMEs do not have the deep pockets and expertise to navigate through the quagmire of antiquated patent processes in multiple foreign countries.

Ironically, this problem disproportionately affects SMEs in the information technology, software, internet, and social media sectors—the new frontier and high growth segments that support many of the best paying jobs.

These respondents reflect a general consensus that procedural reform, not direct subsidization by the U.S. taxpayers, is the principal remedy for the challenges faced by small businesses in obtaining international patent protection.

b. The U.S. Government should approach the direct subsidizing of foreign patenting costs with care.

The comments were split about, but mostly disapproved of, certain kinds of public financial assistance, including loans and grants, from the U.S. government to private industry, but expressed receptiveness to other forms of financial assistance. One industry organization opposed government funding but supported tax incentives:[83]

> The Federal Government should [not] become involved with subsidizing the filing, maintaining, and enforcing of patents abroad. These are private sector issues that are best addressed by businesses, whether large or small. Nonetheless, it may be useful to study the benefit to small enterprises and to the nation of tax breaks for the cost of obtaining patent protection abroad. Also of interest would be profits made through licensing foreign patent rights abroad and the sale of products or services abroad that are covered by such patent rights. In a similar vein, the U.S. Government may consider strategies to encourage sales abroad, for example, by allowing patent costs to be expensed rather than capitalizing them.

A legal practitioner with nearly 30 years of experience working with hundreds of businesses, mostly small companies, opposed government loans categorically and disfavored other forms of assistance:[84]

> I do not endorse a government loan program to help businesses get foreign patents. I oppose government loan programs generally, as I believe the private sector does a better job at evaluating the risks of a loan.

By comparison, a legal practitioner in information technology with over 22 years of experience distinguished loans and grants funded by tax revenues and those funded by user fees, and opposed both:[85]

> A government loan or grant, funded from taxpayer dollars or a portion of existing USPTO user fees, for the purpose of foreign patent procurement by SMEs, does not represent good policy. (a) It would represent, to at least some extent, a redistribution of

---

[83] Comments of American Intellectual Property Law Association, at 7–8, *available at* http://www.uspto.gov/aia_implementation/ipp-2011nov08-aipla.pdf.

[84] Comments of Paul Overhauser, at 2, *available at* http://www.uspto.gov/aia_implementation/ipp-2011oct27-overhauser-paul.pdf.

[85] Comments of Christopher Palermo, at 2–3, *available at* http://www.uspto.gov/aia_implementation/ipp-2011nov01-palermo-christopher.pdf.

U.S. income into the social welfare programs of foreign countries with only speculative benefit to SMEs due to the subjective nature of obtaining patents. . . . (b) Further, a material percentage of SMEs either fail or have limited-vision management: C-level executives who are incapable of growing the company or pursuing products with a limited or immature market. It may be difficult for government to determine which SMEs merit a loan or grant. (c) Finally, it seems fair to place at least some of the burden of financing SME patents on the large entities that dominate the system and, because of their ability to pay high official fees, file large numbers of cases, and wait out the resulting backlog periods involved in foreign patenting, must be seen to contribute to the costs faced by SMEs in the system. For all these reasons, I disfavor a government loan or grant program.

However, opinion was not one-sided. An industry organization invited government support building on existing small business programs:[86]

> For our small businesses, securing IP protection is as important as obtaining laboratory equipment, leasing space, or hiring creative, dedicated employees. And because IP business assets are at least as important as other, more tangible business assets, there is no reason to exempt patent rights from publicly-funded small business assistance programs that are available for more tangible assets such as capital equipment, hiring, or leasing space. Extending the range of public assistance programs to patent rights for small businesses would help small biotechs spend money normally allocated to patent filing and prosecution elsewhere.

These comments reflect the IP community's diverse positions on government support for foreign patenting by small businesses. Even those who oppose government aid oppose it to different extents and for different reasons. Nevertheless, the comments do also reflect a point of consensus: a need for greater education for small businesses on IP in general and foreign patenting in particular.

c. The U.S. Government should pursue an aggressive program of education for small businesses on foreign patenting.

Many respondents and witnesses argued that what small businesses, start-up firms, and independent inventors want from the U.S. government is not capital. Instead, to facilitate more informed acquisition of international patent protection, respondents suggest that greater education about the importance of international patents and ways to obtain them is necessary. One industry organization reported as follows:[87]

> In another area, the USPTO and other Federal agencies can do a much better job educating small businesses about the importance of international patents and strategies for effectively pursuing international protection.

A multinational U.S. law firm with a significant intellectual property practice reported as follows:

---

[86] Comments of Biotechnology Industry Association, at 3, *available at* http://www.uspto.gov/aia_implementation/ipp-2011oct20-bio.pdf.

[87] Comments of American Intellectual Property Law Association, at 5, *available at* http://www.uspto.gov/aia_implementation/ipp-2011nov08-aipla.pdf.

We believe that the key to spurring competitiveness in small business is education about the role international patent protection can play. Rather than fund particular industries/companies, we believe that the U.S. Patent and Trademark Office (PTO) should continue to provide educational workshops/seminars in addition to information on its website. Those should be held through regional small business organizations in order to provide the most direct impact.

10.   In continued response to the questions presented by Congress, the USPTO offers some observations regarding loan programs and grant programs.

Consistent with public commentary, the USPTO does not recommend using public funding to directly support – through either loans or grants – small business international patenting at this time. To be responsive to Congress, however, and as background, it is noteworthy that whether a patent subsidy program is structured as a grant or a loan has implications for how effective it will be, and for what kinds of recipients it reaches. A grant—provided it is limited to supporting expenses associated with filing small-business international patent applications—would provide immediate capital to be used only for obtaining foreign patent protection. Because such capital would be available with no repayment obligation, any eligible small business that is interested could take advantage, so long as it had the resources available to obtain and administer the grant internally. As a matter of basic economics, if the grant covers 100 percent of the expenses associated with international patenting, an over investment in such activity might occur.

In order to combat this possibility, grants are commonly offered with requirements that the awardee invest company capital in some kind of matching scheme, thus investing its own capital in some percentage to the grant capital. This percentage need not be equal shares. So, a grant may be designed to cover only some fraction of the total cost of an activity, and in that way, encourage investment by the business without supporting frivolous or trivial expenditures. Such a grant scheme would tend to support an activity that the government has concluded is desirable, while avoiding the harshest outcomes of government money being used to support activities that have nearly zero private value. Such a matching requirement, however, may affect small businesses disproportionately since—as was discussed previously—small and particularly young companies may not have sufficient cash flow or capital to take advantage of this type of grant scheme in the early years of patenting when such expenditure is necessary.

A loan program can also provide up-front funding, but in contrast to a grant, comes with an obligation to repay the capital later, ordinarily with some interest rate. Loan programs can differ across several dimensions, such as how much capital is available, how long a repayment horizon the recipient will be allowed, and in both the rate(s) of interest and the interval(s) at which interest payments will be due. A government-supported loan program is often economically equivalent to a combination of an ordinary, private loan with an economic subsidy or grant. The subsidy represents the extent to which the loan is more attractive than privately available options, such as offering a means of borrowing more money than otherwise possible, or being allowed a more attractive interest rate or repayment date. In this way, a government-supported loan program can share the attributes of a grant program with a matching requirement. Each presents some kind of subsidy to the small business, but also requires some liability. The main difference comes when that liability is realized. In a grant program, it is realized immediately, while in a loan program, it will be realized after some delay. Also, since loans present the possibility of default if the business fails or is otherwise unable to pay, that liability may not be realized by the small business at all. Since loans consist in part of the borrower's own future assets, the borrowers will be less likely to use them to acquire low-value investments. Thus, loans also present a solution, like matching, to the problem presented by a 100 percent grant.

The question of what type of program is better intersects with problems of uncertainty characteristic of the patenting and innovation process described earlier in this report. A patent is generally filed early in the innovation process when uncertainty is likely high concerning both technological and market potential. Without full information, a small business can underinvest in activities which would be valuable, or overinvest in those which turn out to offer poor returns.

Economic scholars appear to have not devoted significant attention to the value of grants compared to loans to help small businesses with international patenting. Although evidence-driven studies would be a preferred way to compare the policies, a literature review found no analysis that directly compared the effectiveness of loans and grants for a program of the kind described here. So, while the USPTO does not advocate using federal funds for these purposes currently, it must also be recognized that we lack sufficient data to adequately understand whether grants, or loans, or neither mechanism, would be effective.

B.   Recommendations

1.   **The U.S. Government should engage in diplomacy and harmonization to reduce the costs associated with filing foreign patent applications.**

Consistent with public comments received, USPTO recommends that the United States continue to engage our foreign trading partners in efforts to reduce patenting costs faced by American small-businesses abroad.   The lack of small-entity discounts in most of the world's patent offices discourages U.S. small businesses from patenting abroad while at the same time USPTO's small entity discounts encourage foreign small businesses to file in the U.S. Moreover, efforts made toward substantive harmonization of patent laws around the world can aid U.S. small businesses by allowing them to economize on the costs of filing and fulfilling requirements in different offices around the globe.

2. The USPTO and SBA should partner in an expanded IP education and training initiative aimed at American small businesses.

This report's findings support the notion that many small businesses may benefit from extending patent rights outside the U.S., but too few are aware of the need to do so, or the pathways and mechanisms that are available to make these decisions accurately and pursue them cost effectively. Consistent with commentary received from the public, many small businesses would benefit from training in how IP protection and enforcement can be relevant to a growing company in a global economy. Piracy, counterfeiting, and the theft of intellectual property pose a serious threat to many American businesses, whether operating inside or outside the United States.

The USPTO and the SBA are positioned to build upon several successful current IP education and training programs aimed at small businesses, and increase the availability, penetration, and participation in these programs across the United States. The USPTO currently offers a number of tools and training events to assist and train small businesses about their foreign patenting opportunities and obligations. The SBA, too, has networks and resources in the small business community to reach the relevant audience. Moreover, the USPTO has previous experience partnering with SBA, as well as with other U.S. government agencies that work to support the needs of small businesses in internationalization, such as the Minority Business Development Agency and the International Trade Administration.

One notable program that the USPTO has conducted for over five years is the Intellectual Property Awareness Campaign (IPAC). This program provides day-long training sessions in various cities throughout the U.S focusing on intellectual property "basics" including patents, trade secrets, trademarks, domain names, and copyright protection and enforcement, both within the U.S. and abroad. The program is directed at small to medium-sized enterprises (SMEs), which often lack the training, knowledge, and resources possessed by larger companies. Because the USPTO offers the program on request in a web-based seminar format, this training can be tailored to the IP issues most critical to a particular type of small business. The web-based format also enables to the USPTO to reach many more small businesses in a manner, and at a time and place, which suits their needs. In 2011, the IPAC program had over one hundred attendees in various cities throughout the U.S. The IPAC education programs were delivered in person by teams of 4–6 USPTO staff per program.

The USPTO has considerable experience with developing and delivering educational outreach programs in partnership with other U.S. Government institutions. The USPTO's current partners include the SBA; bureaus of the Department of Commerce including the Minority Business Development Agency and the International Trade Administration; and the U.S. Intellectual Property Enforcement Coordinator at the White House Office of Management and Budget. The USPTO has also worked with the U.S. Chamber of Commerce and the National Association of Manufacturers to educate small businesses about domestic and foreign IP protection through on the StopFakes.gov campaign, administered by the International Trade Administration. Not least, the USPTO has developed university partnerships, such as the IP Empowerment Summit at Howard University to educate minority-owned small businesses about domestic and international intellectual property law.

Ideally, any USPTO-SBA education and training program would be scalable so that it may reach more small businesses. One approach to expanding IP education and training for small businesses would be to increase the scale of the current IPAC program, using partnership arrangements and thereby increasing participation by small businesses. That could be accomplished by using electronic resources (such as internet based webinars) and by using physical locations such as the SBA-funded Small Business Development Centers (SBDC) (900 service locations) and the Patent and Trademark Resource Centers (79 locations) around the United States. Other non-government partners could be enlisted. The USPTO and SBA would be responsible for developing materials and training local businesses on day-long or modular small-business foreign patenting content. The USPTO and SBA could conduct more webinars with the existing infrastructure, and leverage the training materials already developed for the IPAC, as well as other patent-relevant courses, to reach larger audiences of small businesses.

Alternatively, the USPTO and SBA could partner, through the SBDCs, to expand upon the services that the SBDC's 900 locations currently provide to small businesses. While the SBDC currently provides training and counseling services to small business throughout the U.S., the USPTO and SBA could "train-the-trainer" so that local staff could deliver relevant materials on international IP protection, and its relation to internationalization strategies of small businesses, to a more diverse and larger segment of U.S. small businesses. These training sessions could be either in-person training or web-based distance learning. The goal would be to educate and train a significantly larger number of U.S. small businesses per year than the IPAC is currently able to reach.

3.   The USPTO and SBA should engage industry to discuss how best to support U.S. small business efforts to patent internationally.

Several comments recognized that small businesses are a part of a larger economic ecosystem, and often engage, partner, and form alliances with different-sized companies at different stages of the innovation cycle and during their internationalization process. Often small companies enter into business relationships, including research and development alliances or distribution agreements across industries. Larger companies, too, often serve as investors in young startup companies through corporate venture capital. The health of the small business sector can be an important determinant of industry success, especially in those industries like pharmaceuticals and electronics that use acquisition of small businesses to fuel large-company innovation cycles.

Because many members of the public expressed a preference for market solutions over direct government intervention, it would be useful and informative for the USPTO, the SBA, and other allied agencies to convene discussions among industry representatives and small-business investors on small business foreign patenting.

4.   **The USPTO and SBA should collect more information and conduct more study on the most appropriate methods of supporting international patenting by small businesses.**

Public commentary – from a small sample of eighteen sources – voiced uncertainty about the advisability of the U.S. government becoming involved in subsidizing small business foreign patenting in a manner that would alter the operation of efficient market solutions. Moreover, there is virtually no evidence, either from academic research or from respondents, about the relative advantages of a loan versus a grant scheme as each relates to defraying the expenses of small businesses seeking international patent protection. Because too little meaningful data could be found relating to the advisability of the U.S. government using taxpayer funds either as a loan or a grant program to support this activity, USPTO does not recommend any program of public financing of small business foreign patenting at this time. However, it would be useful and informative as a next step for the USPTO, the SBA, and other allied agencies to collect more data.

As a general matter, the United States is stronger when we make investments in building the analytical capacity necessary to study the innovation economy. Intangible assets such as patents have been shown in one recent economic study to comprise over 50 percent of all U.S. business outputs,[88] and our capacity as a nation and government to analyze and make sense of these new sources of American national competitive advantage is vital to our long term economic health. The relative paucity of useful information and meaningful analysis concerning key questions that Congress asked the USPTO and SBA to study indicates that more investment in basic understanding of important questions related to American competitiveness in the innovation economy may be desirable. Meaningful policy evaluation requires both the best data and the best analytical capabilities focused on the important questions concerning how America will win the future.

Given the lack of information regarding the questions posed by Congress in the legislation, follow-up surveys and economic studies may be conducted to provide the legislature with the best information upon which to base its policy choices. Surveys targeted to America's small businesses, both those that currently use the patent system as well as innovating small companies that are opting out of the patent system, can provide useful information about their understanding of the value of international

---

[88] *See* Carol Corrado et al, *Intangible Capital and U.S. Economic Growth*, 55 REV. INCOME & WEALTH 661 (2009).

patenting and the utility of different means of providing support. Moreover, economic studies focusing on the relative advantages of choosing grant programs or loan programs, or other approaches to supporting international patenting for those small companies that need that need this protection may be helpful.

Pilot programs too can be an effective means of gathering information when issues are complex, and when there is considerable uncertainty about the benefits that may flow from the use of different possible policies. The USPTO has determined that further study is needed on these issues. In the near term the USPTO does not recommend that a new pilot program of support for international patenting be instituted, thereby avoiding additional burden on taxpayers until more information is gathered.

IV.   CONCLUSION

America's economic health is now and will continue to be determined by the health of America's small businesses. Because many small businesses rely on patent protection to thrive and grow, it is important to understand the relationship between success in the global economy and foreign patenting protection. Foreign patent protection can preserve valuable options for innovative U.S. small businesses to internationalize, to grow, and to become the job creators of tomorrow. The set of proposed recommendations contained in this report is a first responsive step toward better serving U.S. small businesses while gaining a better understanding of the needs and incentives of America's small business entrepreneurs with respect to international patent protection.

www.ingramcontent.com/pod-product-compliance
Lightning Source LLC
Chambersburg PA
CBHW081244170526
45165CB00009B/3182